Brands We Know

John Deere

By Sara Green

Bellwether Media • Minneapolis, MN

Jump into the cockpit and take flight with **Pilot books**. Your journey will take you on high-energy adventures as you learn about all that is wild, weird, fascinating, and fun!

This edition first published in 2016 by Bellwether Media, Inc.

No part of this publication may be reproduced in whole or in part without written permission of the publisher.
For information regarding permission, write to Bellwether Media, Inc.,
Attention: Permissions Department,
5357 Penn Avenue South, Minneapolis, MN 55419.

Library of Congress Cataloging-in-Publication Data

Green, Sara, 1964- author.
 John Deere / by Sara Green.
    pages cm. -- (Pilot: Brands We Know)
 Summary: "Engaging images accompany information about John Deere. The combination of high-interest subject matter and narrative text is intended for students in grades 3 through 7"-- Provided by publisher.
 Includes bibliographical references and index.
 ISBN 978-1-62617-348-4 (hardcover : alk. paper)
1. Deere, John, 1804-1886--Juvenile literature. 2. Deere & Company--History--Juvenile literature. 3. Industrialists--United States--Biography--Juvenile literature. 4. Plows--United States--History.
5. Farm tractors--United States--History. 6. Agricultural machinery industry--United States--History--Juvenile literature. I. Title.
 HD9486.U6D4337 2016
 338.7'6817631092--dc23
 [B]
                    2015028674

Printed in the United States of America, North Mankato, MN.

JOHN DEERE

Table of Contents

What Is John Deere?

A field of corn stretches long and wide. The corn is ready for harvest. A farmer climbs into a bright green combine harvester. This is a John Deere machine. The combine gathers the corn and separates the kernels. Then it shoots them into a grain cart. After a long day, much of the corn is harvested. Next, the corn must be dried. A John Deere corn dryer gets the job done!

Deere & Company, often known as John Deere, makes the John Deere **brand** of products. Company **headquarters** is in Moline, Illinois. John Deere products are used on farms and construction sites. Others are used to cut trees. Many people mow grass with John Deere lawn machines. The company's leaping deer **logo** is recognized around the world. It has been used on John Deere products for about 140 years. People trust the John Deere name. Today, it is one of the most admired businesses in the world.

By the Numbers

worth
$30 billion
in 2015

more than
59,000
employees
worldwide

**400 gallons
(1,514 liters)**
of diesel fuel held by the
9620R tractor

300,000
Model A
tractors built

more than
5 million
diesel engines made

combine
harvester

A Talented Blacksmith

John Deere was born on February 7, 1804, in Rutland, Vermont. When John was 17 years old, he became an **apprentice** to a **blacksmith**. He learned how to make tools and worked at various shops in Vermont. Soon, he was married with a growing family. John was a skilled blacksmith. However, he was not earning enough money. It was time for a change.

John Deere

In 1836, John moved to Grand Detour, Illinois, where he opened his own blacksmith shop. His family soon followed. The local farmers kept John busy making and repairing tools. At that time, farmers used horses to pull iron or wooden plows through soil. However, the plows often got stuck in the thick, sticky dirt. John knew soil would easily slide off steel. This gave him an idea. John reshaped an old steel saw into a curved plow. When he first tested the plow in a field, it cut through the soil with ease! John had invented the first self-polishing steel plow. By 1837, the plow was ready for farmers to use.

re-creation of John Deere's historic blacksmith shop in Grand Detour, Illinois

JOHN DEERE, PROP

Word quickly spread about John's steel plow. He and a partner began making them in John's blacksmith shop. Demand for the plows was high. By 1846, they were making 1,000 plows per year.

The Trade Mark of Quality Made Famous by Good Implements
1910s–1930s tagline

Moline Plow Works ESTABLISHED 1847. Compliments of DEERE & COMPANY January 1st 1882.

Not long after, John sold his half of the blacksmith shop to his partner. The Deere family then moved to Moline, Illinois, to start a new company. There, the Mississippi River provided waterpower. Moline's railroad gave John a way to ship plows and **import** materials. John's company quickly grew. In 1853, John's son, Charles, joined him in the business. Soon, they were selling around 10,000 plows a year.

Ups and Downs

The name of the business officially became Deere & Company in 1868. John and Charles ran the company together. The company soon added wagons, **cultivators**, and other types of farm equipment to its product line. Sadly, John died in 1886. But Charles continued to expand the company. He opened new **branches** and increased production. For a few years, the company even made bicycles!

However, John Deere has not always been a successful business. The **Great Depression** was one of the company's worst times. Sales dropped sharply, and many John Deere workers lost their jobs. Farmers could not pay for John Deere equipment. But the company still cared about its workers and farmers. It helped workers pay their rents and gave them health care. Farmers were allowed to use equipment they did not buy. This generosity paid off. People knew they could trust the John Deere name. When the Depression ended, the company came back stronger than ever.

It's A Combine Man's Dream Come True

1950s tagline

War Service

During World War II, John Deere made parts for tanks and aircrafts. It also made ammunition and mobile laundry units.

John Deere wagon

Top-Selling Tractors

Tractors have played an important role in John Deere's history. The company's first tractors were expensive, so they did not sell well. In 1918, the company began making Waterloo Boy tractors. These affordable tractors were among the first to run on gasoline rather than steam. Many people wanted to buy them.

John Deere continued to make other popular tractors. The Model D was the first to carry the company name. The GP, Model A, and Model B followed, each showing improvements over the last. Tractors became more powerful. They had rubber tires and smoother steering. By 1958, John Deere was the leading tractor maker around the globe.

Model A tractor

Model D tractor

GPS

Today, John Deere tractors are among the world's most popular farm machines. People know them by their bright green color and yellow trim. Most tractors have large, powerful **diesel** engines. These allow them to pull heavy loads. Many drivers sit in enclosed cabs with heat and air-conditioning. **GPS** navigation helps farmers plan exact routes through their fields. Some cabs even have small refrigerators!

GEAR UP!

The John Deere Pavilion

The John Deere Pavilion opened in Moline, Illinois, in 1997. Visitors can learn about the company's history there. They can also see how products work and climb up on big machines.

An Industry Leader

John Deere achieved huge success with its tractors. The company's other products have also made it an industry leader. Many farmers depend on John Deere combines to harvest crops. Farmers also rely on a wide variety of John Deere **implements** that allow tractors to do different tasks. Some implements plow soil or plant seeds. Others apply **fertilizer** or make bales of hay.

At construction sites, John Deere excavators dig holes or move heavy objects with large, strong shovels. The company's dozers push dirt or rocks from one place to another with large metal blades. Front-end loaders scoop up dirt, rocks, and other heavy items.

Loggers use John Deere machines to slice tree trunks. One popular machine is the feller buncher. Its name comes from what it does. The machine fells, or cuts down, trees and then piles them in bunches!

feller buncher

Signature Colors
John Deere's farm, forestry, and lawn care machines are painted green with yellow trim. The company's construction machines are painted yellow with black trim.

John Deere Machines

Machine	Where It Is Used	What Does It Do?
Combine	Farm	Harvests grain crops
Cotton Picker	Farm	Collects cotton from fields
Forage Harvester	Farm	Cuts and gathers grasses and other plants
Seed Drill	Farm	Plants seeds in soil
Tractor	Farm	Pulls farm machines and implements
Dozer	Construction	Pushes materials with a large blade
Excavator	Construction	Digs soil from the ground with a large shovel
Grader	Construction	Smooths roads and other surfaces
Loader	Construction	Moves materials from one place to another
Skid-steer	Construction	Loads and moves heavy materials
Feller Buncher	Forest	Cuts down trees and piles them in bunches
Forwarder	Forest	Picks up, loads, and hauls logs to the road
Harvester	Forest	Cuts trees into logs
Skidder	Forest	Pulls logs over rough ground

forage
harvester

loader

forwarder

John Deere is known for its **innovations**. Engineers often use customer suggestions to make equipment more efficient and comfortable. This has helped John Deere win many awards. The company also seeks ways to save fuel and reduce **emissions**. This way, operators save money and protect the environment.

Nothing Runs Like A Deere

1970s-present tagline

A Powerful Tractor

The John Deere 9620R tractor is one of the largest tractors ever built by the company. Its powerful engine allows the tractor to pull a dump truck three times its weight!

Tango E5

R-Gator

John Deere makes other exciting products. The John Deere Machine Sync allows machines to share information wirelessly. This helps two or more machines, such as seed planters, work more efficiently. They will not overlap routes as they move through fields. The company also makes robots! The R-Gator is a driverless vehicle used by the United States military. It carries supplies and patrols areas to keep troops safe. The Tango E5 lawn mower is another robot. It cuts grass by itself in rain or shine.

John Deere Around the World

The world's population is growing. The need for food, roads, and buildings is also increasing. John Deere is ready for the challenge. Today, the company has offices and factories in more than 30 countries. This allows the company to provide equipment and technology where it is needed.

John Deere is also committed to fighting world hunger. In 2014, the company's **foundation** gave nearly $32 million to **charitable** organizations. Many of them teach farming skills to people in Africa and Asia. Farmers learn how to **conserve** soil and water. Some programs give modern equipment and technology to farmers to help them grow more crops. John Deere also helps farmers buy seeds, **pesticides**, and other products necessary for growing crops.

Company employees make a difference, too. Many **volunteer** at local food banks and schools. Others travel overseas to help farmers harvest crops. Through its commitment to people, farms, and communities, John Deere helps improve lives around the world.

Golfing for Good

Each year, famous golfers compete in the John Deere Classic in Illinois. This tournament began in 1971. Since then, it has raised more than $61 million for charity!

John Deere Timeline

1804
John Deere is born in Rutland, Vermont, on February 7

1837
John makes the first self-polishing steel plow in Grand Detour, Illinois

1848
John moves to Moline, Illinois, where he opens his business

1868
The business is officially named Deere & Company

1858
John's son, Charles, takes control of the business

1876
The leaping deer logo is first used

1886
John passes away in Moline, Illinois, on May 17

1918
Deere & Company
buys Waterloo
Boy tractors

2014
John Deere is named one
of the 50 most admired
companies by *Fortune*
magazine

1971
The slogan "Nothing
Runs Like A Deere" is
introduced

1943
The company builds
military machines for
World War II

1927
The first John Deere
combine is built

1964
World Headquarters
opens in Moline,
Illinois

1998
For the first time,
John Deere's net
earnings reach
$1 billion

1949
John Deere debuts
the Model R, its first
diesel-powered tractor

2012
John Deere
celebrates 175 years
as a company

Glossary

apprentice—a person who works for a more skilled person in order to learn a trade

blacksmith—a person who makes things from iron or steel

branches—locations away from company headquarters where business is done

brand—a category of products all made by the same company

charitable—helping others in need

conserve—to use carefully in order to prevent loss or waste

cultivators—tools that break up soil and uproot weeds

diesel—a type of engine in which heat from compressed air lights fuel

emissions—dangerous fumes

fertilizer—a chemical that helps plants grow

foundation—an institution that provides funds to charitable organizations

GPS—global positioning system; a GPS device finds locations and gives directions from one place to another.

Great Depression—a time in world history when many countries experienced economic crisis; the Great Depression began in 1929 and lasted through the 1930s.

headquarters—a company's main office

implements—tools that have certain tasks and are often attached to machines

import—to bring in from another country

innovations—new methods, products, or ideas

logo—a symbol or design that identifies a brand or product

pesticides—chemicals that kill insects

volunteer—to do something for others without expecting money in return

To Learn More

AT THE LIBRARY

Alexander, Heather. *Big Book of Tractors*. New York, N.Y.:
Parachute Press, DK Pub., 2007.

Mason, Helen. *Agricultural Inventions: At the Top of the Field*.
New York, N.Y.: Crabtree Pub. Co., 2014.

Sutcliffe, Jane. *John Deere*. Minneapolis, Minn.: Lerner
Publications, 2007.

ON THE WEB

Learning more about John Deere
is as easy as 1, 2, 3.

1. Go to www.factsurfer.com.

2. Enter "John Deere" into the search box.

3. Click the "Surf" button and you
   will see a list of related web sites.

With factsurfer.com, finding more information
is just a click away.

Index